Time in the Garden
Walking in the Power of Prayer

Book Eight

Walking with Jesus

Becoming the Best Me I Can Be

Pamela D White

All scripture quotations, unless otherwise indicated, are taken from the Holy Bible, **New King James Version©**. Copyright © 1982 by Thomas Nelson, Inc. Used by permission. All rights reserved.

Scripture quotations marked NIV are taken from the Holy Bible, **New International Version** ®, NIV ®. Copyright © 1973, 1978, 1984 by **Biblica, Inc.® Used by permission. All rights reserved worldwide.**

Scripture quotations marked NASB are taken from the Holy Bible, **New American Standard Bible®,** Copyright © 1960, 1971, 1977, 1995, 2020 by The Lockman Foundation. All rights reserved.

Scripture quotations marked AMP are taken from the Holy Bible, **Amplified**, copyright © 2015 by The Lockman Foundation, La Habra, CA 90631. All rights reserved. For Permission To Quote information visit http://www.lockman.org/

Scripture quotations marked ESV are taken from the ESV® Bible (The Holy Bible, **English Standard Version**®). ESV® Text Edition: 2016. Copyright © 2001 by Crossway, a publishing ministry of Good News Publishers. The ESV® text has been reproduced in cooperation with and by permission of Good News Publishers. Unauthorized reproduction of this publication is prohibited. All rights reserved.

Scripture quotations marked NLT are taken from the Holy Bible, **New Living Translation**, copyright © 1996, 2004, 2015 by Tyndale House Foundation. Used by permission of Tyndale House Publishers, Inc., Carol Stream, Illinois 60188. All rights reserved.

Scripture quotations marked MSG are taken from **THE MESSAGE**, copyright © 1993, 2002, 2018 by Eugene H. Peterson. Used by permission of NavPress. All rights reserved. Represented by Tyndale House Publishers, Inc.

Scripture quotations marked AKJV are taken from the Holy Bible, **Authorized King James Version**, The Authorized (King James) Version of the Bible ('the KJV'), the rights in which are vested in the Crown in the United Kingdom, is reproduced here by permission of the Crown's patentee, Cambridge University Press. The Cambridge KJV text, including paragraphing, is reproduced here by permission of Cambridge University Press.

A publication of Blooming Desert Ministries

ISBN 978-1-7370803-4-3 (sc print)
ISBN 978-1-7370803-5-0 (ebook)

Printed in the United States of America
Copyright © 2021 by Pamela D White
All Rights Reserved.

IngramSparks Publishing (Ingram: Lightning Source, LLC)

One Ingram Blvd., La Vergne, TN 37086

Publishing Note: Publishing style capitalizes certain pronouns in Scriptures that refer to the Father, Son, and Holy Spirit, and may differ from other publishing styles. **All emphasis in the Scriptures' quotations is the authors.** The name satan and related names are not capitalized as the author's preference not to acknowledge him, even though it violates grammatical rules.

No part of this book may be reproduced or transmitted in any form or by any means, electronic or mechanical – including photocopying, recording, or by any information storage and retrieval system – without permission in writing from the publisher. Please direct inquires to PDW Publications.

Dedication

This book series is dedicated to you.

Everyone has opportunities to become a better version of themselves. My prayer is that this book series helps you on that journey. The Lord loves you so much He desires an intimate relationship with you. You are special to Him and He loves spending time with you. Walking and talking with Jesus every day should be the norm, not the exception. Life can bring difficult circumstances and situations. When you walk with Jesus, life events, are not only manageable but can be turned for your good.

"And we know that all things work together for good to those who love God, to those who are the called according to His purpose," Romans 8:28.

Come with me into this exploration of how you can develop a relationship with Jesus and walk with Him every day. This is an opportunity to become a better you.

Acknowledgments

The Great Commission given by our Lord and Savior Jesus Christ noted in Matthew 28:16-20 is my inspiration for this publication. Verses 19-20 state, *"Go therefore and make disciples of all the nations, baptizing them in the name of the Father and of the Son and of the Holy Spirit, teaching them to observe all things that I have commanded you; and lo, I am with you always, even to the end of the age."* This verse is the very basis for missionary work all over the globe. I have been blessed to be able to serve in a few of those missions. Missions are an amazing experience. I came to realize though that everyone cannot always do all the parts commanded in these verses. I can't always go. I didn't often get to baptize. What I realized was that I can do my part in teaching to observes the truths of the Scriptures. My desire to fulfill the teaching part of the Great Commission was the inspiration for this work. My pastor, Bishop Larry Taylor, and First Lady Desetra Taylor allowed our church to use these Bible studies in our New Life Discipleship classes for nearly twenty years. The work has also been used in prison ministries in central Illinois for as many years. The teaching has proven effective in changing many lives and discipling the children of God. Thank you, Bishop and First Lady, for teaching a balanced spiritual and natural life so I could complete this project and see the impact of the work on people's lives.

Bishop positioned me to be the director of New Life Ministries Discipleship for several years. New Life classes were designed to teach those new to Christianity or new to the church the foundational truths needed to build a solid life in Christ. During that time, this work was fine-tuned with the help and input from the dedicated, gifted, and anointed New Life teachers Minister Retta Smith, Minister James Smith, Minister Debby Henkel, Dr. Terry Husband, Minister Char-Michelle McDowell, Minister Yvonne Smith, Minister Herbert Smyer, and Professor Susan Gibson along with the encouragement and guidance of Dr. Chequita Brown and community service advocate Minister Patricia Turner. I also want to give a shout-out to Dr. Wanda Turner, nationally acclaimed minister, teacher, prophet, life coach, mentor, and best-selling author, who continued to encourage me to just publish the thing! Thanks to all of you. Each of you has made a significant impact on my life.

My dear friend and mentor, First Lady Marshell Wickware, supported the project and pushed me to publish it for years. Thanks for not giving up on me!

My life-long friend, Robin McClallen, thank you for all your support, input, and encouraging me to publish something. You have been instrumental in making me an author.

A special thanks to my husband, Brian K. White, for his patience and prayers as I spent hours and hours researching, writing, and rewriting. Thanks, BW!

Most of all thank you to the Holy Spirit and my Lord and Savior Jesus Christ. I present this work in obedience and honor to You.

Contents

Introduction	11
What is Prayer?	13
Why Should I Pray?	17
Heart Posture	19
How Do I Approach God?	23
How Do I Pray?	33
Example of a Journal Entry	37
The Lord's Prayer Model	39
Where Should I Pray?	45
Deterrents to Prayer	49
Does God Hear My Prayer?	53
Example Prayer Journal	55
Stepping Stones	57
Time in the Garden	59
Glossary	61
About the Author	67

Book Eight
Time in the Garden
Walking in the Power of Prayer

OBJECTIVE

This lesson presents a definition of prayer, why prayer is important and provides assistance for how to pray effectively. We will learn about the Lord's Prayer and how to use this model in our daily time with the Lord. Included in this lesson are five steps to hearing God's voice.

MEMORY VERSE

"Do not be anxious about anything, but in everything, by prayer and petition, with thanksgiving, present your requests to God." Philippians 4:6 NIV

"And pray in the Spirit on all occasions with all kinds of prayers and requests. With this in mind, be alert and always keep on praying for all the saints." Ephesians 6:18

Time in the Garden

A. What is Prayer?

B. Why Should I pray?

C. Heart Posture
   1. Spiritual Hearing
   2. Spiritual Taste
   3. Spiritual Scent
   4. Spiritual Emotions, Mind, Will

D. How Do I Approach God?
   1. Humble
   2. With Confession
   3. Confident and Bold
   4. Seeking
   5. Expectant
   6. Faithful
   7. Trusting
   8. Childlike

E. How Do I Pray?
   1. Hearing God's Voice
   2. The Lord's Prayer

F. Where Should I Pray?

G. Deterrents to Prayer

H. Does God Hear My Prayer?

I. G. Prayer Journal Example

Book Eight

Time in the Garden
Walking in the Power of Prayer

Introduction

This lesson will help you to understand the importance of prayer, the impact of prayer on your life, and teach you how to pray and hear God. The Lord desires to spend time with you and talk about what's going on with you as well as to show you who He is and how much He loves you. He desires an intimate relationship with you and prayer is how that happens.

Did God walk in the Garden of Eden with Adam and Eve? Genesis 3:8 implies that Adam and Eve were familiar with the Lord coming to the Garden. They knew the sound of Him approaching. They were not surprised when He showed up. They knew Him well enough to know that the choice they just made would disappoint Him. That says to me that not only did the Lord know Adam but Adam knew the Lord. That is the kind of relationship God desires to have with you. *"And they heard the sound of the Lord God walking in the garden in the cool of the day,"* Genesis 3:8.

What is Prayer?

Prayer is communication with God. It is your direct line to heaven. It is a two-way conversation between you and God. You talk to God; He listens. God talks to you; you listen. Prayer is not complicated. You are to go to God in child-like faith. Prayer is an expression of that child-like faith. Everyone has not had a great relationship with their father, but picture with me if you will a small child coming to their father and making a request. Perhaps it's for a cookie, a piece of candy, a request for a game of hide-and-seek, or reading a book together. It is completely natural for a child to request something from their father. The child asks; the father listens; the father answers and the child replies. It is a two-way conversation. Prayer is as simple as that—a relationship where you have a conversation with the Lord.

Because prayer is part of your relationship, you must first enter the relationship. Receiving Christ into your heart and becoming a child of God gives you the privilege through Jesus Christ of access to the Lord anytime and anywhere. You have the promise that you are never alone.

*"Be strong and courageous. Do not be afraid or terrified because of them, for the L*ORD *your God goes with you; he will never leave you nor forsake you,"* Deuteronomy 31:6 NIV.

"For He Himself has said, "I will never leave you nor forsake you," Hebrews 13:5b.

"I am with you always, even to the end of the age," Matthew 28:20.

These are only a few of the verses where the Lord promises to always be with you—everywhere—all the time. Because He is always with you, He is always available. He doesn't sleep. He is always there. You can talk to Him anytime, day or night.

"My help comes from the Lord, who made heaven and earth. He will not allow your foot to be moved; He who keeps you will not slumber. Behold, He who keeps Israel shall neither slumber nor sleep," Psalm 121:2-4.

Not only is God readily available at all times, but He also promises to answer you when you call Him. He is not a silent God. He created you to spend time with Him. Before Adam's disobedience in Genesis, the Lord would have frequent conversations with him. They talked about many things, just walking and talking like a father and son walking in the garden and chatting about things. When Adam disobeyed, that relationship fractured. Jesus came to repair that relationship, so once again humankind has that open door to walk and talk with the Father. There are many, many scriptures about the readiness of God to speak to His children. I encourage you to dig into your Bible and find what the Lord is saying about conversing with you. The Lord very much wants to talk to you. **HE DESIRES TIME WITH YOU** and the opportunity to be intimate with you. He knows everything about you. After all, He made you. He knows your heart better than you do. Nothing you say to Him surprises Him, and He will answer you when you call Him. He doesn't block you, unfriend you, ignore you, junk mail you, or delete you. He will always be there.

"He shall call upon Me, and I will answer him; I will be with him in trouble; I will deliver him and honor him," Psalm 91:15.

"It shall come to pass that before they call, I will answer; and while they are still speaking, I will hear," Isaiah 65:24.

"Ask, and it will be given to you; seek, and you will find; knock, and it will be opened to you. For everyone who asks receives, and the one who seeks finds, and to the one who knocks it will be opened. Or which one of you, if his son asks him for bread, will give him a stone? Or if he asks for a fish, will give him a serpent? If you then, who are evil, know how to give good gifts to your children, how much more will your Father who is in heaven give good things to those who ask him!" Matthew 7:7-11 ESV.

Matthew 7 sums up what prayer is pretty well.

1. Prayer is communicating with God—both talking and listening.

2. Prayer is making requests known by faith.

3. Prayer is asking and receiving.

4. Prayer is seeking and finding.

5. Prayer is knocking and experiencing God's openness.

Why Should I Pray?

Prayer is an acknowledgment that God is God. He is all-powerful, Lord of lords and King of kings. God knows everything and there is nothing He can't do. Recognizing these truths will bring you to an intimacy with God that is unsurpassable. Here is a small sampling of scriptures that show several benefits gained when you pray.

1. *"Then He spoke a parable to them, that men always ought to pray and not lose heart,"* Luke 18:1. To lose heart is to be completely and utterly exhausted. Ever been there? Prayer will keep you from losing heart.

2. *"Watch and pray, lest you enter into temptation. The spirit indeed is willing, but the flesh is weak,"* Matthew 26:41. You still live in a body that has to live with a fallen world. Temptation is all around and will come seeking you. Prayer will give you the strength to resist temptations.

3. *"Whoever calls on the name of the Lord shall be saved,"* Romans 10:13. God is a God of salvation. When you call on Him, His great love always responds.

4. *"If any of you lacks wisdom, let him ask of God, who gives to all liberally and without reproach, and it will be given to him,"* James 1:5. God does not want you ignorant of His ways. When you ask Him for wisdom, God is faithful to supply and supply abundantly.

5. *"Until now you have asked nothing in My name. Ask, and you will receive, that your joy may be full,"* John 16:24. Joy is a by-product of answered prayer.

6. *"Yet you do not have because you do not ask,"* James 4:2. Did you ask Him yet? Maybe you don't have it because you haven't asked for it yet! God takes delight in answering your prayers. You can talk to Him about anything. He's waiting for you to come to talk and tell Him what you need and want. He promises to give you the desires of your heart. Just talk to Him about it.

7. *"This poor man cried out, and the Lord heard him, and saved him out of all his troubles,"* Psalm 34:6. Trouble will come. It's inevitable. When you call on God, He will deliver you out of them all. The last time I checked 'all' means all!

8. *"Moreover, as for me, far be it from me that I should sin against the Lord in ceasing to pray for you; but I will teach you the good and the right way,"* 1 Samuel 12:23. Prayer helps keep you in right standing with the Lord and helps you teach others the good and right way.

9. *"Call to Me, and I will answer you, and show you great and mighty things, which you do not know,"* Jeremiah 33:3. The Lord has many secret things. They are only secret from those who do not know Him. As His child, He desires to show you the hidden truths. Just ask Him. He says if you call to Him, then He will answer. Trust that He will answer you and show you amazing revelation.

Heart Posture

Prayer expresses worship, praise, reverence, and faith. It is a spiritual action, which comes from your heart. You have physical senses that help you interpret the physical world. Eyes see, ears hear, noses smell, tongues taste, skin feels. Your spiritual being has senses that mirror the five physical senses. Actually, it's the other way around. Your physical body's senses mirror your spiritual senses. God created you with spiritual eyes, spiritual ears, a spiritual sense of smell, spiritual taste, and spiritual emotions. You can walk around your entire life and never use your spiritual senses. When you develop a relationship with the Lord, those spiritual senses awaken and you see, hear, and feel in a whole new way.

Spiritual Sight:

"Having the eyes of your hearts enlightened, that you may know what is the hope to which he has called you, what are the riches of his glorious inheritance in the saints," Ephesians 1:18 ESV.

"To open their eyes, so that they may turn from darkness to light and from the power of Satan to God, that they may receive forgiveness of sins and a place among those who are sanctified by faith in me," Acts 26:18 ESV.

"Then the eyes of the blind shall be opened, and the ears of the deaf unstopped; then shall the lame man leap like a deer, and the tongue of the mute sing for joy," Isaiah 35:5-6a.

SPIRITUAL HEARING:

"Whoever is of God hears the words of God. The reason why you do not hear them is that you are not of God," John 8:47 ESV.

"But he said, "Blessed rather are those who hear the word of God and keep it!" Luke 11:28 ESV.

SPIRITUAL TASTE:

"Taste and see that the Lord is good; blessed is the one who takes refuge in him," Psalm 34:8.

"And have tasted the good word of God and the powers of the age to come," Hebrews 6:5.

"How sweet are Your words to my taste, sweeter than honey to my mouth," Psalm 119:103.

SPIRITUAL SCENT:

"For we are to God the fragrance of Christ among those who are being saved and among those who are perishing.," 2 Corinthians 2:15.

"Therefore be imitators of God as dear children. 2 And walk in love, as Christ also has loved us and given Himself for us, an offering and a sacrifice to God for a sweet-smelling aroma," Ephesians 5:1-2.

Spiritual emotions, mind, will:

"I say then: Walk in the Spirit, and you shall not fulfill the lust of the flesh...But the fruit of the Spirit is love, joy, peace, longsuffering, kindness, goodness, faithfulness, gentleness, self-control," Galatians 5:16, 22-23.

"Teach me to do Your will, for You are my God; Your Spirit is good. Lead me in the land of uprightness," Psalm 143:10.

"And to be renewed in the spirit of your minds," Ephesians 4:23 ESV.

There are many more scriptures about your spiritual senses. In Book One – *There Must Be a Better Way*, we discussed that you are a three-part being: spirit, soul, and body. You are a spirit that has a soul and lives in a body. Life begins with your body senses ruling your life—I'm hungry, I'm thirsty, I'm hot, I'm cold, etc. You need those physical senses to function in the physical world. When the Spirit of God enters your life, your spirit awakens and you begin to use your spiritual senses. You need those spiritual senses to function in the spiritual world. The Spirit of God will show you things and speak things to you. To see and understand what He is showing you and to hear what He is speaking; you need your spiritual senses.

"When the Spirit of truth comes, he will guide you into all the truth, for he will not speak on his own authority, but whatever he hears he will speak, and he will declare to you the things that are to come. He will glorify me, for he will take what is mine and declare it to you. All that the Father has is mine; therefore I said that he will take what is mine and declare it to you," John 16:13-16 ESV.

How Do I Approach God?

The best way to approach the Lord is with a **HUMBLE** heart. He is the Creator and Lord of all. You are His creation. Prayer is an acknowledgment that God is higher and more powerful than you. He rules the universe, sees all things, knows all things, and is everywhere at all times. God knows you better than you know you. He has answers to questions you haven't even thought of yet. It is important to acknowledge that He is who He says He is.

"Humble yourselves before the Lord, and he will exalt you," James 4:10 ESV.

"If My people who are called by My name will humble themselves, and pray and seek My face, and turn from their wicked ways, then I will hear from heaven, and will forgive their sin and heal their land," 2 Chronicles 7:14.

"I will bless the Lord at all times; His praise shall continually be in my mouth. My soul shall make its boast in the Lord; the humble shall hear of it and be glad. Oh, magnify the Lord with me, and let us exalt His name together," Psalm 34:1-3.

Come clean or expecting to get clean. You can come to God at any time with anything. He is a 'come as you are' God because He loves you. He knows you mess up, and He knows you make bad decisions sometimes. Still, He wants you to come to Him. The weight of those poor decisions and negative circumstances is heavy and burdensome. When you come to Him with those things, His will is to relieve you of that burden. He wants you to dump that at His feet. The Spirit will help you get cleaned up, mend broken places, and heal your wounds. Sometimes that means **CONFESSING** sin. Again, God is not surprised by anything you bring to Him. He saw you do it! Not only that but He heard the thoughts that brought you to make that decision. Remember, God is with you always. Nothing you say to Him is a shocker. He just wants to help you clean up and relieve you of your burdens, dressing you in His righteousness, and give you strength and courage to not make that negative decision again. Then your prayers have significant power, and next time you will make a better decision because whatever caused you to make that bad decision was healed, so now you can make a godly, righteous decision.

"If we confess our sins, he is faithful and just to forgive us our sins and to cleanse us from all unrighteousness," 1 John 1:9 ESV.

"Therefore, confess your sins to one another and pray for one another, that you may be healed. The prayer of a righteous person has great power as it is working," James 5:16 ESV.

"Come to Me, all you who labor and are heavy laden, and I will give you rest. Take My yoke upon you and learn from Me, for I am gentle and lowly in heart, and you will find rest for your souls. For My yoke is easy and My burden is light," Matthew 11:8-30.

You can approach the Lord **CONFIDENT AND BOLD**. In the Old Testament, the only one who could enter the Holy of Holies was the High

Priest. No one else had the privilege of speaking to the Lord one-on-one. Then Jesus came and died for you, so that barrier was no longer there. God gave visual confirmation the barrier was gone when the veil partitioning the Holy of Holies from the people ripped from top to bottom. When Jesus died and rose from the dead, He gave you full access to speak to God anytime. Jesus now serves as the High Priest and invites you to enter the throne room of God with full access. When you believe Jesus is who He says He is, you can confidently approach the Lord.

"Let us therefore come boldly to the throne of grace, that we may obtain mercy and find grace to help in time of need," Hebrews 4:16.

"In whom we have boldness and access with confidence through our faith in him," Ephesians 3:12 ESV.

"Therefore, brothers, since we have confidence to enter the holy places by the blood of Jesus," Hebrews 10:19 ESV.

When approaching the Lord, you want to come **SEEKING** Him. That might sound silly because why would you go to someone and not be looking for them, right? But it happens all the time. People's prayers are a grocery list of things they need help with. They recite the list, then leave the list at the door and never have a conversation with the One they are asking to fulfill the list. The Lord wants a relationship with you, not a list of demands or requests. He will take your list, but most of all He wants time with you. He wants you to search for Him. When you spend time with Him, all those things on your list are just taken care of. Much more important than your list is developing a relationship with the Lord. He loves you and wants to spend time with you and helping you get to know Him better. Nothing on your list is more important than growing in your relationship with the Lord. That doesn't mean you can't ask the Lord for your needs. He is more than willing to hear those requests. He just wants to fulfill those needs through your relationship with Him rather than have you drop off your list and go on your way.

"But from there you will seek the Lord your God and you will find him, if you search after him with all your heart and with all your soul," Deuteronomy 4:29 ESV.

"Ask, and it will be given to you; seek, and you will find; knock, and it will be opened to you. For everyone who asks receives, and the one who seeks finds, and to the one who knocks it will be opened," Matthew 7:7-8 ESV.

"But seek first the kingdom of God and his righteousness, and all these things will be added to you," Matthew 6:33 ESV.

"I love those who love me, and those who seek me diligently find me," Proverbs 8:17 ESV.

When talking to the Lord, be **EXPECTANT**. Believe that He hears you and understands. Believe that He sees your need and expect He will answer. Expect goodness, mercy, grace, and kindness. The religious world often portrays God as a punishing God who reigns with terror and fear; or a God who is indifferent to your needs; or a God who has forgotten you. The Scriptures however paint a much different picture of God. God is good and He does good always. *"You are good and do good; teach me your statutes,"* Psalm 119:68. He promises to never leave you, so there is no way He can forget you because He is with you at all times. *"Can a mother forget her nursing child, and not have compassion on the son of her womb? Surely they may forget, yet I will not forget you,"* Isaiah 49:15. The Lord gets angry at sin, but He never stops loving you. He loves you so radically He sent His Son to die in your place, just so He could restore relationship with you. *"For God so loved the world that He gave His only begotten Son that whosoever believes in Him should not perish, but have everlasting life,"* John 3:16. You should also expect change. Change in your situation and/or change in you. He is always helping you to renew your mindsets, so every day you can increasingly know more of who He is. *"Therefore, preparing your minds for action, and being sober-minded, set your hope fully on the grace that will be brought to you at the revelation of Jesus Christ,"* 1 Peter 1:13. Since God is a good God who hears and sees and walks with you, you can ask Him expecting an answer and expecting help. Nothing is too hard for Him and nothing surprises Him. He will give you strength, hope, joy, love, faith, and so much more. He is a God of endless resources. There is no task He cannot accomplish. So you can approach the Lord with great expectancy.

"For with God nothing will be impossible." Luke 1:7.

"Therefore I say to you, whatever things you ask when you pray, believe that you receive them, and you will have them," Mark 11:24.

"I can do all things through Christ who strengthens me," Philippians 4:13.

"Now this is the confidence that we have in Him, that if we ask anything according to His will, He hears us," 1 John 5:14.

The word of God says in Hebrew 11:1 that faith comprehends as fact what you cannot see or experience yet in the physical. Faith is like a title deed to everything that is divinely guaranteed. Praying in **FAITH** means that even if it seems impossible, if God said it, you can believe it. Faith empowers you to speak what the Word says is true, believe what the

Word says, receive what the Word says and act on what the Word says. Let me give you an example. I mentioned some strange things happening to my doctor. Within hours, the doctors diagnosed me with a brain tumor. The doctors had a very negative prognosis. I could have believed what they were telling me, but in faith, I believed the Word of God instead. 1 Peter 2:24 says, *"who Himself bore our sins in His own body on the tree, that we, having died to sins, might live for righteousness—by whose stripes you were healed."* I believe the Lord healed me. I could see the tumor on the MRI scans. I could feel the symptoms of a brain tumor. I could hear the doctor's diagnosis. Those were all things in the physical world. I chose in faith to believe what I knew God had said. God had healed me. I spoke healing scriptural truths. I believed God had already accomplished this for me, received the truth that God is a healer, and believed He had healed me. I acted on that word by thanking the Lord for His healing and told others about my healing. I went to all the doctor's appointments, reminding the doctors that though I would do what they said, the Lord was the Great Physician that healed me. As I write this, I'm healed and I no longer have a brain tumor. Speak it, believe it, receive it, and act on it. When life hits hard, find a scripture that will refute the negatives of the world, say it out loud and tell your supportive friends, believe it even when the reports are negative, receive it and thank God that His word is true, and act on it by showing the Lord your gratefulness. That is praying in faith.

"And without faith it is impossible to please him, for whoever would draw near to God must believe that he exists and that he rewards those who seek him," Hebrews 11:6.

"So Jesus answered and said to them, "Have faith in God. For assuredly, I say to you, whoever says to this mountain, 'Be removed and be cast into the

sea,' and does not doubt in his heart, but believes that those things he says will be done, he will have whatever he says. Therefore I say to you, whatever things you ask when you pray, believe that you receive them, and you will have them. And whenever you stand praying, if you have anything against anyone, forgive him, that your Father in heaven may also forgive you your trespasses," Mark 11:22-25.

Partnered with faith is **TRUST**. The Lord never leaves you and He hears all your prayers. The Lord is all-powerful and all-knowing. God is love. He has all knowledge and understanding. The Lord has a path prepared for you. He is everything you need at all times. When your strength is waning and your spirit is fainting, when you are just too tired to know what to do, when life is overwhelming, when making it through one more day seems like an overwhelming task—He is the Rock you can lean on. The Lord is your hope and He is your good reward. God is your strength and protector. He is there for you. When you pray, trust that He is your answer.

"And those who know your name put their trust in you, for you, O Lord, have not forsaken those who seek you," Psalm 9:10.

"Trust in the Lord with all your heart, and do not lean on your own understanding. In all your ways acknowledge him, and he will make straight your paths," Proverbs 3:5-6

"The Lord is my strength and my shield; in him my heart trusts, and I am helped; my heart exults, and with my song I give thanks to him," Psalm 28:7.

God is Father. He created you. It is because of Him you exist. Psalm 139 tells how He knit you together in your mother's womb. He knows everything about you and He wants you to come to Him as His child because He is Abba Father. That does not mean childishness. To be childish is to be selfish and immature. Childish behavior is annoying in an adult and unacceptable behavior. To be childlike speaks of innocence and humility. To be **CHILDLIKE** is to trust the Lord humbly and love Him unconditionally. Childlike speaks of purity and goodness. You are to come to the Lord humbly and expectantly as a child approaches a father. He is a Father who loves His children, and He desires to give His children good gifts. You can approach Abba Father with the assurance that He will receive you, His child, with a warm and loving embrace.

"Truly, I say to you, unless you turn and become like children, you will never enter the kingdom of heaven. Whoever humbles himself like this child is the greatest in the kingdom of heaven," Matthew 18:3-4 ESV.

"Truly, I say to you, whoever does not receive the kingdom of God like a child shall not enter it," Luke 18:7 ESV.

"Therefore be imitators of God, as beloved children," Ephesians 5:1 ESV.

"Beloved, now we are children of God; and it has not yet been revealed what we shall be, but we know that when He is revealed, we shall be like Him, for we shall see Him as He is," 1 John 3:2.

Having an attitude of thanksgiving is very important. Every breath you take comes from Him. Your cells function because of Him. You exist because of Him. Every good and perfect gift comes from Him. He is everything. He is all in all. He is worthy of thanksgiving and praise. Coming to the Lord in prayer should always include thanksgiving. **THANKSGIVING** should drip from your mouth all day long. When you thank Him for even the smallest things, your entire attitude changes and faith builds. Thank Him for what He does: He became your salvation, redeemed you, and made you His own. Thank Him for who He is: good, just, faithful, deliverer, redeemer, salvation, rock, high tower, refuge, righteousness, peace, joy, love, healer, provider and so much more. Thank Him for what He gives: love, grace, mercy, rest, peace, and victory. The lists are so long, there is no way to list them all here. It would take volumes of books that the whole world cannot contain to list all of who God is and what He does. Thank Him.

"Enter his gates with thanksgiving, and his courts with praise! Give thanks to him; bless his name!" Psalm 100:4 ESV.

"Be anxious for nothing, but in everything by prayer and supplication, with thanksgiving, let your requests be made known to God," Philippians 4:6

"Continue earnestly in prayer, being vigilant in it with thanksgiving," Colossians 4:2.

"Therefore by Him let us continually offer the sacrifice of praise to God, that is, the fruit of our lips, giving thanks to His name," Hebrews 13:15.

How Do I Pray?

There is nothing you cannot talk to God about. He wants to be involved in every aspect of your life. God understands your weaknesses and temptations. He also understands your needs and desires. Prayer isn't just about asking God for the things you need to help you in situations or asking the Lord to intervene in situations. Prayer is about developing a relationship with the Lord. Have you ever entered a relationship where you called and text each other day and night? Maybe you stayed up late talking on the phone? You thought about them when you weren't with them, missing them when you were apart. You talked about everything: how you feel, what you want, your desires and dreams, your favorite things, your history, your future, what happened yesterday at work and so much more. That's what prayer is about. Jesus wants to talk to you about everything! He wants to be your best friend and the easiest way to develop that relationship is through prayer.

Maybe you never heard prayer like that before? Or didn't know you could talk to the Lord and have him talk back to you like that? Here is how to develop a relationship with the Lord that is as easy as talking to your best friend. Mark Virkler has several books teaching these steps such as "4 Keys to Hearing God's Voice." The keys taught by Mark Virkler are based on Habakkuk 2:1-2

"I will stand my watch and set myself on the rampart, and watch to see what He will say to me, and what I will answer when I am corrected. Then the Lord answered me and said: "Write the vision and make it plain on tablets, that he may run who reads it."

Here are five steps on how to develop your relationship with the Lord and enter into a conversation with Him.

1. Be **STILL**. Quiet yourself down. If you are not quiet, then you can't hear when God speaks to you. This not only means quieting yourself on the outside but quieting yourself on the inside too. Psalm 46:10 commands, *"Be still, and know that I am God."* You see in this scripture that knowing God is the objective, but to do that, you must be still. Many things can help you learn to be still. One thing that helps me is listening to instrumental worship music. There are a lot of things you can do. Find what works for you.

2. Recognize that God's voice is heard and seen as spontaneous thoughts in your mind. It might sound like your voice because it is in your head, but it is God speaking. The **FLOW** of God might sound like your voice, but it won't sound like how you talk. His voice is much wiser, healing, loving, and encouraging. He sounds gentle and strong. God will speak encouragement, edification, joy, and most of all love. When you listen to the flow of thoughts as you talk to the Lord, you will hear what He is saying to you when you are completely focused on what He is saying.

3. Look for **VISION** as you talk to Him. God will give you pictures in your spiritual imagination. The pictures might be a little hazy or they might be crystal clear. They might be in bold colors or black and white. It doesn't matter. One is not better than another. The

important thing is that your spiritual eyes open and see. The Lord might share a special place where He wants to spend time with you, like a beach or a mountain or maybe just the park across the street. He might show you how He likes to walk with you or do something fun together. The Lord might show you a vision of something He wants to do with you or something about your future or heal you. He wants you to experience things together and a vision is a great place to do that. There are people throughout scripture that had experiences with the Lord through vision. Joseph saved an entire nation from a dream, Moses built a tabernacle, David saw how to build a temple, Joshua got battle strategies and won victories, Philip saw a man desiring prayer and went to him, Peter and Paul both had life-altering visions, and John received the entire book of Revelation—all in dreams and vision. There are so many more. I encourage you to look them up. God is the same yesterday, today, and forever, so if He spoke to so many in the past in visions, then why wouldn't He show you vision as well? He totally will show you a vision. Most of all, He wants to show you how much He loves you. All you have to do is look!

4. Write or **JOURNAL**. Write the thoughts and pictures the Lord gives you. Ask Him questions. Have a conversation. Writing it down helps keep you focused on Him and keeps the conversation flowing. Journaling allows you to record the flow of thoughts, so you can check them with scripture later. It also records any instruction the Lord gives you, so you can go back later and make sure you forget nothing. The Lord is very encouraging. Sometimes it helps just to go back and read something He spoke to you to build your faith. Use a notebook, your computer, or a journal – anything

that allows you to type or write what the Lord is speaking to you and showing you. Don't worry about grammar or punctuation. Just get it down before your mind forgets it.

5. My Pastor frequently reminds us that **REPETITION** creates definition. When you are trying to build muscle, you repeat the exercise several times a week to increase your muscle tone and definition. When you are building your relationship with the Lord, you also need to repeat the exercise of being still, allowing the Spirit to flow, looking for vision, and writing down your conversation. The more you repeat this exercise, the more defined your hearing and vision will become as well as developing and defining a richer and more satisfying relationship with the Lord.

Example of a Journal Entry

I asked the Lord, "How do you feel about me, Lord?"

Dear one, you are the love of My life I cherish my time with you. You are as a prize rose sparkling with dew.

Lord, roses have thorns. I've thought of thorns as hurtful and I don't want to be hurtful. I like the sparkly part though.

Roses do indeed have thorns. Thorns are not meant for deliberate harm, but for protection. You do not deliberately harm. You glisten and sparkle like this rose.

Thank you, Lord. If I am like a rose it is because of You.

I am the Rose of Sharon, My child. The rose has beauty, sweet fragrance, strength, and resilience. Its petals are intricate and vibrant. I am the Rose of Sharon and you are My rose.

What is the glistening dew?

It is the anointing, child. It is new mercies fresh every morning. It brings bounty and blessing. It is My message to come to Me daily for refreshment. The blessing of dew is upon you. Remember, manna came with the dew. Provision and blessing. Nourishment and life. Unconditional blessing. A gift from heaven. Rest in Me, child. Rest in My blessing and pro-

vision and allow the beauty of who I have created you to bring pleasure to those around you and draw them to Me. Rest in Me.

Then the Lord led me to this verse:

"I will be like the dew to Israel; He shall grow like the lily, and lengthen his roots like Lebanon. His branches shall spread; His beauty shall be like an olive tree, and his fragrance like Lebanon," Hosea 14:5-6.

You can have a conversation with the Lord like that, too, when you practice these five steps.

The Lord's Prayer Model

Jesus's followers witnessed Him praying every day. One day after Jesus had been praying, one of His disciples said to Him, "Lord, teach us to pray, as John also taught his disciples." Jesus' response to that request was to provide His disciples a model of what prayer looks like. Today, many call this model the Lord's Prayer. It is God's design for prayer and can be found in Luke 11:1-4. Here is the outline of this perfect prayer with some explanations of what it means for you.

The Lord's Prayer

Our Father which art in Heaven, Hallowed be Thy Name.

Prayer should begin with praise, honor, and giving all glory to God. It is only by the sovereign God that you live and move and even exist. He is the Creator of all and Ruler of everything. Therefore, starting prayer by recognizing the Lord's majesty is a great way to begin.

You can use the various names of God to make your faith declarations known to the Lord.

EL SHADDAI "Lord God Almighty"

EL ELYON "The Most High God"

ELOHIM "God"

ADONAI "Lord, Master"

YAHWEH "Lord, Jehovah"

JEHOVAH-TSIDKENU "Jehovah our righteousness"

JEHOVAH-M'KADDESH "Jehovah who sanctified"

JEHOVAH-SHALOM "Jehovah is peace"

JEHOVAH-SHAMMAH "Jehovah is there"

JEHOVAH-ROPHE "Jehovah heals"

JEHOVAH-JIREH "Jehovah's provision shall be seen"

JEHOVAH-NISSI "Jehovah my banner"

JEHOVAH-ROHI "Jehovah my Shepherd"

JEHOVAH-SABAOTH "The Lord of Hosts"

These are only a few of the Lord's names. The Lord has so many more names, they cannot all be listed here – Rose of Sharon, Shepherd, High Priest, Abba Father, and on, and on. The Lord will prompt you on who He is for you each day. Give Him glory for being who He says He is.

Thy Kingdom come, Thy will be done.

Our will can often impede God's will, so pray that it is not your will but God's will that is happening in your life. You want His kingdom to rule and reign, not what you build. His kingdom is much more effective, powerful, restful, and full of grace. Seek Him for His will for you, your family (spouse, children, other family members), your church (pastor, leadership, faithfulness of people, leaders, harvest), and your nation (city, state, and national political and spiritual leaders, and the harvest of souls). You won't pray for all this every day. Let the Lord lead you on what His will is for each day and He will lead you on who to pray for and how to pray His will. He may put a picture or vision of someone in your imagination that He wants you to pray for. He may show you situations that need prayer. Tune into the flow of the Holy Spirit and He will guide your prayers.

GIVE US THIS DAY OUR DAILY BREAD.

What is bread? Bread represents the necessities of life. God is your Provider, so daily ask Him to meet the needs of your day. Every day has needs. He can and will supply those needs when you seek Him.

Bread also represents the Word of God, your spiritual food. Your spirit needs to be fed, too. Giving daily bread means you read and meditate on the Word and open your heart to what the Lord is speaking to you about the Word.

Bread represents people in your life. You were created to need others, and others were created to need you. God often works through people. Chances are high other people will be the help you need today.

Bread represents salvation. The Old Testament tells of the showbread in the temple, which is a representation of the face of God. It is to be in His presence where there is grace, abundance, and prosperity. In the New Testament, Jesus gives communion with bread and wine, showing you His love and sacrifice just for you.

And forgive us our debts/trespasses/sins as we forgive our debtors/trespassers/those indebted to us.

Different churches say this part of the prayer differently so let's look at the original language and see what it means. The word used for debts/trespasses/sins is the Greek word *'hamartia.'* The meaning of *hamartia* provided in Strong's Concordance is to miss the mark, be mistaken, or to wander from God's law. It means the line was crossed. Since the line was crossed, you need to ask the Lord for forgiveness. This passage is not just about asking the Lord's forgiveness for yourself but also that you choose to forgive others who also crossed the line and may have caused you pain and harm. You don't have to be their best friend and you may not need to talk to them, but you need to release them to the Lord in forgiveness. Forgiveness releases them into God's hands so He can deal with the issue, and it releases you so you don't get into anger and bitterness.

Can't think of anything or anyone to forgive today? Ask the Lord what needs addressed and listen for His answer. If something is there, He will show you.

And lead us not into temptation, but deliver us from evil.

Every single day, you will have multiple temptations, which create choices. You can choose doubt or faith, unbelief or belief, eat the candy, or don't eat the candy. The day is full of choices. You need God's help in making righteous decisions and keeping you from the plans of the evil one. God doesn't tempt you. He may allow trials to occur. This part of the prayer is asking God to show you a way out of trials and temptations. He equips you to stand against temptations and gave you the armor of

God for the battle. You can find the armor in Ephesians 6:10-18 (see "Walking Strong"). You can also pray for your protection. Psalm 91 is a great Scripture to declare God's protection.

While you are having this conversation with the Lord, you have the opportunity for Him to drop wisdom into you so you can handle whatever is coming today. How awesome is that?!

FOR THINE IS THE KINGDOM, AND THE POWER, AND THE GLORY FOREVER.

Prayer has come full circle. Once again you give God all glory, honor, and praise. This is your faith declaration and thanksgiving that God is in control. He is all power. His kingdom reigns and you can tell Him so.

The important thing about prayer is that you have a conversation with God. Be still and pay attention. Invite Him to show you things and tell you about things. Allow the fountain of the Holy Spirit to flow through you and thank Him for all His insight into your day. What a great way to start your day!

Where Should I Pray?

The answer to this question is easy. Pray everywhere at all times. You should always listen, tune in for instruction and communication with the Lord. When you have your time with the Lord, it is very helpful to find a place where you can be uninterrupted and is quiet. I use my spare bedroom and sometimes I go to the park or sit on the swing outside. Finding a quiet space is not always possible, so you might have to make some adjustments. The reality is that you can talk to and hear from God anywhere and anytime. Here are a few Scriptures of different places and different situations where people stopped and prayed.

- In Acts 12:1-19 Peter is arrested and put in prison. Scripture doesn't tell us Peter prayed but it does tell us that the church prayed. Their prayers were so effective that an angel was sent to the prison to rescue Peter. Peter got up and walked right out of the prison.

- In Acts 16:16-34, Paul and Silas are thrown into prison because through the power of the Name of Jesus, a servant girl was delivered from demons. Her master was furious and had them put into prison. Paul and Silas began to pray in the darkness of night in the prison. All the prisoners were listening to them when a great earthquake shook the prison violently. The guards were sure they had lost all the prisoners, but Paul assured him that everyone was there. As a result, the prison guard and his whole family received salvation and were baptized.

- Acts 1:13-14 tells of the whole group of believers in Christ gathered together in a room praying and worshiping the Lord. Scripture tells us they were with one accord, one mind, one passion, one purpose. I was at a conference in St. Louis with thousands of believers. We were in a very large coliseum together with one purpose – to meet with the Lord. As we gathered and began to praise the Lord together the power of the passion and being of one mind filled that stadium. There is great power when believers gather and pray with like minds.

- Acts 2:42-47 shows the believers not only going to the temple but meeting together from house to house. They ate and praised the Lord together. This is often called fellowshipping with believers. Shared praise is a form of prayer and as you can see from this passage, it drew many more to the Lord who received His salvation.

- We have just discussed several instances of people gathering together for prayer. It is also important to spend time alone with the Lord. The Lord instructs you to go into your secret place and spend time with Him alone. It's great to socialize and be hospitable with other believers. But just like in a marriage where you need to spend alone time with your spouse, it's important to spend time with your Lord. Just you and Him. Jesus went up into the mountains and stepped away in the garden. If Jesus needed alone time with Father God, how much more do you need alone time.

"But you, when you pray, go into your room, and when you have shut your door, pray to your Father who is in the secret place; and your Father who sees in secret will reward you openly," Matthew 6:6.

- 1 Timothy 2:8 tells you to not only pray everywhere but to pray freely, lifting your hands. You can be on your knees, dance around the room, walk, run, drive a car, in the checkout line at the store, in the shower, painting, prison, or absolutely anywhere. God is everywhere and always ready to listen. Maybe lifting your hands feels weird to you, but try it sometime. It's a humble submission and surrender to the Lord that is very powerful and uplifting. The Lord enjoys physical expressions of your love for Him – singing, dancing, laughing, weeping, lifting your hands, waving a banner, playing an instrument, banging on a pan. He will take your offering of praise and give you creative ways to express your worship.

- As you practice these prayers and become comfortable talking with the Lord, you will find yourself speaking with and hearing the Lord all day long. That's how it's supposed to be! Not only that, you will experience joy in this relationship and develop a grateful heart.

"Rejoice always, pray without ceasing, in everything give thanks; for this is the will of God in Christ Jesus for you," 1 Thessalonians 5:16-18.

Deterrents to Prayer

God is always listening and available to hear your prayers. He does not sleep and never slumbers. The enemy can try to block your prayers or the answer to your prayers, like he tried to block the answer to Daniel's prayers in Daniel 10. You can also cause your prayers to be hindered. Here are a few ways you can block your prayers.

1. **Sin** will always block prayer and hinder you from hearing directions or answers to your prayers. Everybody sins, so don't deceive yourself and say you don't. You do. God knows your sin, and so do you. Confess it and get rid of it.

   "If we say that we have no sin, we deceive ourselves, and the truth is not in us. If we confess our sins, He is faithful and just to forgive us our sins and to cleanse us from all unrighteousness. If we say that we have not sinned, we make Him a liar, and His word is not in us," 1 John 1:8-10.

The following items are all different sins that the Bible reminds us will block communication with the Lord.

2. Selfish or **wrong motives** can block prayer.

"You ask and do not receive, because you ask amiss, that you may spend it on your pleasures," James 4:3

3. **A big prayer blocker is doubt** and unbelief. His will is that you come to Him in faith, believing that He is and does what He says. What you think and believe is huge regarding answered prayer.

   "But let him ask in faith, with no doubting, for he who doubts is like a wave of the sea driven and tossed by the wind. For let not that man suppose that he will receive anything from the Lord," James 1:6-7.

4. Wickedness or **iniquity** in the heart will block your prayers from ever reaching God. Iniquity is repeating sins that are often generational. Example: Grandpa gambled. Dad said he never would, but he gambles too. You said you would not lose the car like dad did and yet… the bank account is empty and you owe gambling debts. That's iniquity – repeated generational sin. Get rid of it.

   "If I regard iniquity in my heart, the Lord will not hear," Psalm 66:18.

   "Behold, the Lord's hand is not shortened, that it cannot save, or his ear dull, that it cannot hear; but your iniquities have made a separation between you and your God, and your sins have hidden his face from you so that he does not hear," Isaiah 59:1-2.

5. Faith is the currency of heaven. **Doubt** is poverty of the spirit. Without faith, things just don't happen. Your account is empty. When you go to the store, if you need something, you need money to buy it. Stealing isn't an option. When you go to God, you need faith to believe He is who He says He is and faith that He hears you and will answer you.

"But without faith it is impossible to please Him, for he who comes to God must believe that He is, and that He is a rewarder of those who diligently seek Him," Hebrews 11:6.

6. **Unforgiveness** will mess you up. The Lord instructs you to love Him and love your neighbor. Unforgiveness isn't His way. You don't have to accept the sin or be besties with the one who hurt you, but you need to place them in God's hands. He will take care of it if you give Him space. You be concerned for yourself and let go of that burden. It's too heavy to carry.

"But I say to you that everyone who is angry with his brother will be liable to judgment; whoever insults his brother will be liable to the council; and whoever says, 'You fool!' will be liable to the hell of fire. So if you are offering your gift at the altar and there remember that your brother has something against you, leave your gift there before the altar and go. First be reconciled to your brother, and then come and offer your gift," Matthew 5:22-24.

7. God has put a model of your relationship with Him on earth. The husband and wife relationship is intended to be a representation of the intimate relationship you are to develop with the Lord. That is one reason the enemy has worked so diligently in destroying this model. Disharmony between husband and wife hinders prayers.

"Likewise, husbands, live with your wives in an understanding way, showing honor to the woman as the weaker vessel, since they are heirs with you of the grace of life, so that your prayers may not be hindered," 1 Peter 3:7 (It would be wise to read verses 1-7 for the full picture.)

Does God Hear My Prayer?

Yes, God hears all prayers. You learned in the previous section that sometimes prayers can be blocked, but that doesn't mean He doesn't hear. It means there is a problem with you not with God. Blocked means you know you should pray but don't. It means you know God is your answer, but you try to fix it yourself. Blocked means selfishness and self-centeredness are more important than seeking God. It doesn't mean God doesn't hear. Blocked means you didn't ask or you didn't ask with the right motives.

The Lord won't hear prayers that come from sin. If there is sin, pray a prayer of repentance. Scripture is very clear that if you are in sin, prayers are not heard. If you feel your prayers are not being heard, then look to see where the sin is and repent! If there is no sin, then He heard you.

The Scriptures speak much about prayer.

"Call to me and I will answer you, and will tell you great and hidden things that you have not known," Jeremiah 33:3 ESV.

"Now this is the confidence that we have in Him, that if we ask anything according to His will, He hears us. Now this is the confidence that we have

in Him, that if we ask anything according to His will, He hears us," I John 5:14-15.

"I cried to him with my mouth, and high praise was on my tongue. If I had cherished iniquity in my heart, the Lord would not have listened. But truly God has listened; he has attended to the voice of my prayer. Blessed be God, because he has not rejected my prayer or removed his steadfast love from me!" Psalm 66:17-20 ESV.

"The Lord is far from the wicked, but He hears the prayer of the righteous," Proverbs 15:29 ESV.

"Before they call I will answer; while they are yet speaking I will hear," Isaiah 65:24 ESV.

"When the righteous cry for help, the Lord hears and delivers them out of all their troubles," Psalm 34:17.

"If you ask me anything in my name, I will do it," John 14:14 ESV.

"The eyes of the Lord are toward the righteous and his ears toward their cry," Psalm 34:15 ESV.

Example Prayer Journal

Date: _____

Lord, I praise you for …

Lord, what would you say to me today?

Lord, forgive me for…

Lord, I lay this at your feet …

Lord thank you for answering my prayer about …

Stepping Stones

1. Prayer is a direct line to God where you both talk and you both listen – communication.

2. The Lord desires time with me.

3. Prayer is a source of encouragement, protection, edification, strength, and love.

4. Prayer is opening my spiritual sensory realm to Jesus.

5. Approach the Lord humbly, confidently, boldly, expectant, seeking, childlike and with faith, trust and thanksgiving.

6. Pray using the five steps to hearing God's voice and He will always respond.

7. The Lord gave me a model of prayer to follow using the Lord's Prayer.

8. I can pray anytime and anywhere.

9. Sin blocks communication with the Lord.

10. God will show me secret, hidden things when I meet with Him faithfully.

Time in the Garden

WALKING IN THE POWER OF PRAYER

1. Describe how prayer is communication between you and God.

2. Name the 5 steps to hearing God's voice giving a short description of each.

    a. _____

    b. _____

    c. _____

    d. _____

    e. _____

3. What changes do you need to make in your prayer life?

4. What names of God have had an impact on your life? Thank Him!

Glossary

SIMPLE GLOSSARY OF A FEW WORDS FROM THE CHRISTIAN FAITH

Adultery - The act of being sexually unfaithful to one's spouse

Agape - Affection, goodwill, love, brotherly love, a love feast

Angel - Messenger of God

Apostasy - Turning away from the religion, faith, or principles that one used to believe

Apostle - One sent forth, one chosen and sent with a special commission as a fully authorized representative of the sender.

Atonement - To cover, blot out, forgive; restore harmony between two individuals.

Attribute – An inherent characteristic

Backslide - To go back to ungodly ways of believing or acting.

Blasphemy - Words or actions showing a lack of respect for God or anything sacred.

Bless - To make or call holy, to ask God's favor, to praise; to make happy.

Blessing - A prayer asking God's favor for something, something that brings joy or comfort.

Born-again – To be begotten or birthed from God, the beginning, to start anew

Carnal - Of the flesh or body, not of the spirit, worldly; seat of one's desires opposed to the spirit of Christ

Cherubim - Guardian angels, angels that guard or protect places

Commitment - A promise, a pledge

Conditional - Placing restrictions, conditions, or provisions to receive

Conversion - Turn, return, turn back; change

Convert - To change from one form or use to another, to change from one belief or religion to another.

Courtship - The act or process of seeking the affection of one with the intent of seeking to win a pledge of marriage

Covenant - A pledge, alliance, agreement

Cult - A body of believers whose doctrine denies the deity of Christ.

Deliverance - A freeing or being freed, rescue; the act of change or transformation.

Demon - Evil spirit

Devil - Principal title for satan, the archenemy of God and man

Dispensation - A period of time, sometimes called ages

Dominion - To rule over, have power over, overcome, exercise lordship over

Eros - Erotic, physical love

Eternal - Existing always, forever, without time

Evangelist - Proclaims the gospel of Jesus Christ

Faith - Believing, trusting, depending, and relying on God

Fellowship - Sharing, communion, partnership, intimacy

Forgiveness - To pardon, release from bondage

Fornication - To act like a harlot, to be unfaithful to God, illicit sexual intercourse

Glorification - Salvation of the body, transforming mortal bodies to eternal bodies

Grace - Unmerited favor of God, help given in the time of need from a loving God

Holy - Set apart, sacred

Intercession - To meet or encounter, to strike upon, to pray for another

Justification - Salvation of the spirit, just as if I never sinned

Marriage - A divine institution designed by God as an intimate union, which is physical, emotional, intellectual, social, and most importantly, spiritual

New Testament - Text of the new covenant

Offering - Everything you give beyond your tithe

Old Testament - Text of the old covenant

Omnipotent - All-encompassing power of God

Omnipresent - Unlimited nature of God, ability to be everywhere at all times

Omniscient - God's power to know all things

Pastor - Shepherds of the body of believers

Philia - Conditional love, based on feelings, friendships

Praise - Thanksgiving, to say good things about, words that show approval.

Prayer - Communication with God

Prophet - One who is a spokesperson for God, one who has seen the message of God and declares that message

Propitiation - To satisfy the anger of God, to gain favor; appease

Rapture - To be carried away, or the catching away of

Reconciliation - Restore harmony or fellowship between individuals, to make friendly again

Redemption - To buy back, to purchase, recover, to Rescue from sin

Regeneration - To give new life or force to, renew, to be restored, to make better, improve or reform, to grow back anew

Repent - To give new life or force, to renew, to be restored, to make better, improve or reform, to grow back a new.

Resurrection - A return to life subsequent to death

Revelation - The act of revealing or making known

Righteousness - Right standing with God, integrity, virtue, purity of life, correctness of thinking

Sacrifice - The act of offering something, giving one thing for the sake of another; a loss of profit

Salvation - Deliverance from any kind of evil whether material or spiritual, being saved from danger or evil; to rescue.

Sanctification - Salvation of the soul. Separation from the seduction of sin

Satan - The chief of fallen spirits, opponent; adversary

Sealing - Something that guarantees, a sign or token, to make with a seal to make it official or genuine

Sin - All unrighteousness, missing the mark, wrong or fault; violation of the law

Spirit - A being that is not of this world, has no flesh or bones

Steward - A guardian or overseer of someone else's property, manager

Supernatural - Departing from what is usual, normal, or natural to give the appearance of transcending the laws of nature

Talent - A natural skill that is unusual.

Tithe - Ten percent of all your increase

Tribulation - Distress, trouble, a pressing together, pressure, affliction

Trinity - Three in one: Father, Son, Holy Spirit

Unconditional - No restrictions, conditions, boundaries, demands, or specific provisions

Will – Choice, inclination, desire, pleasure, command, what one wishes or determines shall be done

About the Author

Pamela is a teacher, mentor, and author of the inspirational book *Destiny Arise* and children's books including *Time in a Tuna*. Pam earned her bachelor's degree at the University of Illinois Springfield, her master's degree in Organizational Leadership at Lincoln Christian University, and her doctorate in Leadership at Christian Leadership University. She serves as a mentor for the Spirit Life Circles sponsored by CLU.

She works from her home in the prairie land of central Illinois. Pam and her bodybuilding husband own a gym/fitness center that promotes living a balanced life. She taught sixth grade for almost twenty years. Pam also taught preschool through adult-age students in various venues. She served as director of Super Church, the children's ministry in the United Methodist Church in her hometown. Pam also served in the church nursery, as director of New Life Ministries Discipleship Program, Vacation Bible School Director, Kingdom Kids Children's Ministry Director, and Sunday School teacher. She has also been on missionary trips. Her favorite trip, so far, was the time she spent in Belize.

Pam enjoys kayaking, bicycling, and riding her motor scooter. When she isn't writing, she enjoys spending time with her four children and their families which includes five grandchildren who are the inspiration of her children's books.

Walking with Jesus Series

Becoming the Best Me I Can Be

Book 1 - There Must Be a Better Way
Walking in Salvation

Book 2 - Lord, I Need Help!
Walking with the Holy Spirit

Book 3 - I Thought I Was Changed
Walking in Transformation

Book 4 - I Am Supernatural
Walking in Spiritual Gifts

Book 5 - I Am Strong
Walking as a Warrior

Book 6 - I Am Fruitful
Walking in the Fruit of the Spirit

Book 7 - Love Letters from God
Walking in the Word

Book 8 - Time in the Garden
Walking in the Power of Prayer

Book 9 - I'm in Charge of What?
Walking in Stewardship

Book 10 - The End of – Well, Pretty Much Everything
Walking into Eternity

Who am I? What am I doing here? Where am I going? Everyone at some point in life asks these questions. You were wired to ask and engineered to pursue the answers. The road to discovering destiny is besieged by fiascoes, failures, and the agony of defeat. If your strength has been depleted and has caused you to give up, sit down, push pause, and snooze until another day, then this book is just for you! Amazing experiences are waiting for you. Get ready to be awakened from the posture of defeat, depression, and despair.

Destiny Arise is an easy-to-read book, providing tools to aid in living an amazing life. This book is designed as a trip adviser for your expedition. It will teach you how to evict the spirit of mediocrity and use your past to propel you into your future. You will learn how to shake off the common, arising to be an uncommon force taking your rightful place in the earth. You can change the world. I pray this book will ignite a passionate fire to pursue your destiny unapologetically. Destiny, awake from your slumber and arise.

www.ingramcontent.com/pod-product-compliance
Lightning Source LLC
Chambersburg PA
CBHW062155100526
44589CB00014B/1848